GEORGE WASHINGTON CARVER

SCIENTIST, INVENTOR, AND TEACHER

SPECIAL LIVES IN HISTORY THAT BECOME

Signature LIVES

GEORGE WASHINGTON CARVER

SCIENTIST, INVENTOR, AND TEACHER

by Michael Burgan

Content Adviser: Gary R. Kremer, Ph.D.,
Executive Director,
State Historical Society of Missouri

Reading Adviser: Rosemary G. Palmer, Ph.D.,
Department of Literacy, College of Education,
Boise State University

Compass Point Books Minneapolis, Minnesota

Compass Point Books
3109 West 50th Street, #115
Minneapolis, MN 55410

Visit Compass Point Books on the Internet at *www.compasspointbooks.com*
or e-mail your request to *custserv@compasspointbooks.com*

Editor: Jennifer VanVoorst
Page Production: Noumenon Creative
Photo Researcher: Svetlana Zhurkin
Cartographer: XNR Productions, Inc.
Library Consultant: Kathleen Baxter

Art Director: Jaime Martens
Creative Director: Keith Griffin
Editorial Director: Carol Jones
Managing Editor: Catherine Neitge

Library of Congress Cataloging-in-Publication Data
Burgan, Michael.
George Washington Carver : scientist, inventor, and teacher / by Michael Burgan.
p. cm. — (Signature lives)
Includes bibliographical references and index.
ISBN-13: 978-0-7565-1882-0 (library binding)
ISBN-10: 0-7565-1882-2 (library binding)
ISBN-13: 978-0-7565-1986-5 (paperback)
ISBN-10: 0-7565-1986-1 (paperback)
1. Carver, George Washington, 1864?–1943—Juvenile literature.
2. African American agriculturists—Biography—Juvenile literature.
3. Agriculturists—United States—Biography—Juvenile literature. I. Title.
II. Series.
S417.C3B88 2007
630.92—dc22 [B] 2006027072

Printed in the United States of America.

Signature Lives

MODERN AMERICA

Starting in the late 19th century, advancements in all areas of human activity transformed an old world into a new and modern place. Inventions prompted rapid shifts in lifestyle, and scientific discoveries began to alter the way humanity viewed itself. Beginning with World War I, warfare took place on a global scale, and ideas such as nationalism and communism showed that countries were taking a larger view of their place in the world. The combination of all these changes continues to produce what we know as the modern world.

Table of Contents

Chapter

1 The Peanut Man Emerges

On a hot September afternoon in 1920, George Washington Carver stood before a room full of white people in Montgomery, Alabama. Carver, an African-American scientist, inventor, and teacher, had been born a slave. Even though slavery had ended more than 50 years earlier, racism was still strong across the United States, especially in the South. The people Carver addressed, a reporter later wrote, had "doubts ... as to the advisability of having one of the negro race come before them." But Carver's words—and more important, the items he had brought with him to Montgomery—soon won over his doubting audience.

The crowd that day was made up of members of the United Peanut Association of America. The peanut growers were looking for ways to increase

Known as the Peanut Man, George Washington Carver displayed the many different products that could be made from peanuts.

their sales. They also hoped the U.S. government would place a tariff on foreign peanuts to make them more expensive than U.S. peanuts. With a lower price, American peanut growers could sell more of their product. Now, the peanut growers hoped Carver could help their cause.

In the years after slavery ended in 1865, many states—especially in the South—passed laws to segregate African-Americans and whites. Blacks had their own waiting rooms at train stations and their own cars on trains. Black and white children attended separate schools, and African-Americans could not eat at "white" restaurants. Segregation laws were often called Jim Crow laws. They were named after a character in a traveling music show. During the 1830s, a white actor began darkening his face and making fun of slaves by singing a silly song and dancing wildly onstage. Soon other whites performed as this character known as Jim Crow.

Getting into the meeting hall that day had not been easy for Carver. At first a worker refused to let him into the hotel where the meeting was taking place. Carver finally convinced the man to take a note to the peanut growers, letting them know he was there. When Carver was allowed into the hotel, he was forced to use the freight elevator, rather than the elevator used by white customers. Carver, like other blacks of the time, lived under the Jim Crow laws of the South, which segregated whites and blacks. Carver, however, never showed anger about racism, and he had many close friends who were white.

When he reached the hotel's

meeting room, Carver set down a suitcase he had brought with him from Tuskegee, Alabama. He had taught at the all-black Tuskegee Institute since 1896. There, in his small laboratory, he had conducted experiments on the peanut. Carver was convinced that growing peanuts would help Southern farmers. The peanut was easy to raise and added nitrogen to the soil. Nitrogen helped keep the soil healthy, so other crops could be grown after the peanuts were harvested. Carver also worked long hours to discover new products that could be made from peanuts. Now in Montgomery, he amazed the peanut growers with some of his findings.

Georgia peanut farmers picked peanuts from their vines in the 1920s.

The peanut was first grown in South America. European explorers and soldiers saw Native Americans eating the seeds of the peanut plant—what are commonly known as the nuts. From South America, the Europeans brought the plant to Africa, where it grew easily and became an important part of the diet. African slaves took peanuts with them when they were brought to North America. They were the first people to raise peanuts in what became the United States, growing them in their own small gardens. Goober, a nickname for the peanut, comes from the West African word nguba*, which was used by slaves in the South.*

Using his long, thin fingers, Carver took out several dozen bottles. Some held stains that could dye leather or wood different colors. Other bottles were filled with things to drink, such as coffee and cream. Everything, he explained, was made from peanuts.

To Carver, his most important peanut product was peanut milk. He once called peanut milk "delicious and wholesome." He told the peanut growers how 3 ounces (84 grams) of raw peanuts could be turned into 1 pint (.47 liters) of milk. Carver's peanut milk was packed with protein. It could be produced in regions of the world where farmers had trouble raising dairy cows. Making peanut milk was also faster than getting milk from a cow. "It takes the cow twenty-four hours to make milk," Carver told a reporter in 1921. "I can make from peanuts better, cleaner and more healthful milk in five minutes."

Carver's talk dazzled the peanut growers. They voted to help him gain patents for his products. The reporter who noted the audience's doubts about Carver when he first walked in said, "Dr. Carver ... won his way into the hearts of the peanut men."

The growers might have been "peanut men," but soon Carver was known as the Peanut Man.

George Washington Carver conducted many experiments in his laboratory at Tuskegee Institute.

The peanut belongs to the legume family, which includes peas and beans.

Newspapers and magazines began writing about him and his many uses for the peanut—more than 300 in all. In 1921, the United Peanut Association of America asked Carver to promote their interests in Congress.

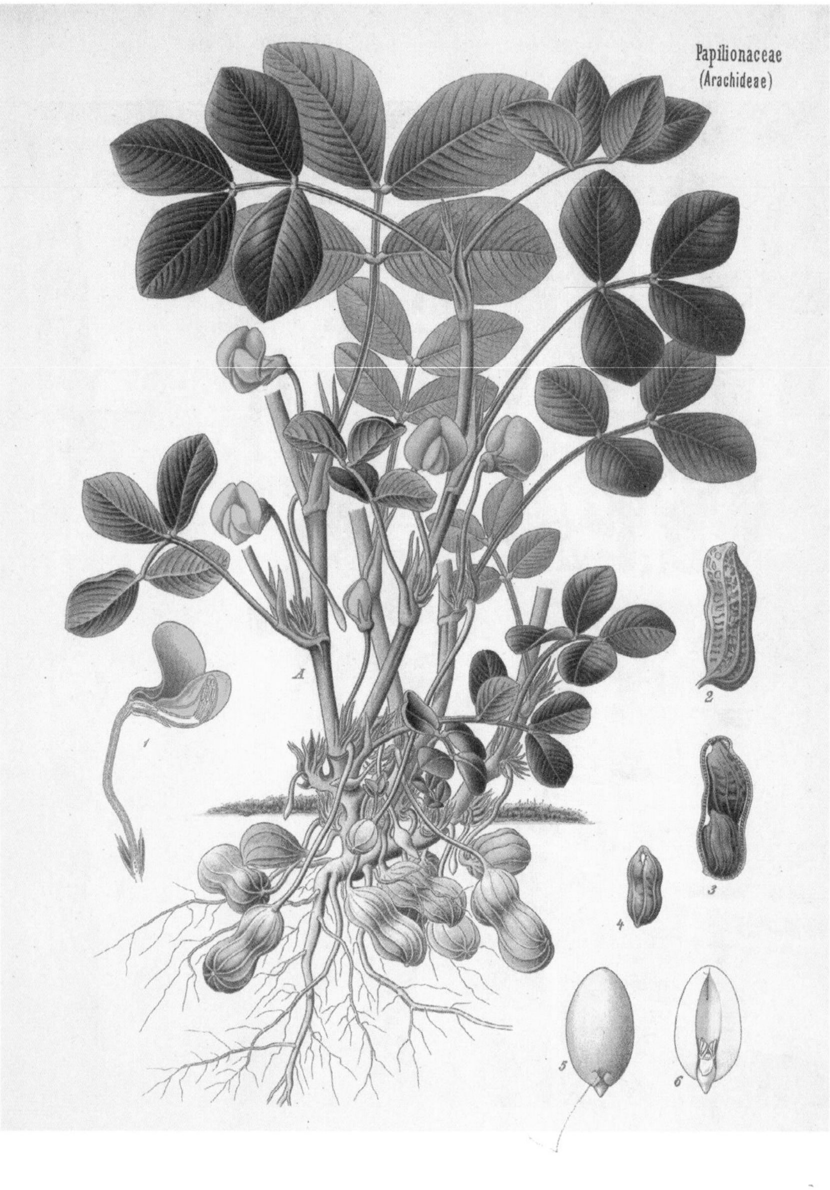

The gentle scientist used his knowledge and sense of humor to persuade the U.S. lawmakers to give the peanut growers the tariff they wanted.

In the years that followed, Carver's fame continued to grow. Although he was usually associated with the "goober," he was more than just the Peanut Man. In his lab and on the farm, he studied a variety of crops. He looked for ways to improve soil and help farmers grow more crops on each acre. In the classroom, he encouraged students to do their best. Carver was also a deeply religious man. He called his lab "God's Little Workshop" and gave God credit for his success. Carver believed God wanted humans to use nature wisely and not waste the products of the earth.

Carver's life became a great example of what African-Americans could achieve. His work showed that blacks possessed intelligence and natural talents—traits some whites thought they lacked. He also showed that hard work helped bring those talents into the world to help others.

Chapter 2 From Slavery to Freedom

Few people who knew George Washington Carver as an infant would have guessed the fame that awaited him. Carver entered the world as the son of slaves at a time when Southerners were fighting to defend their right to own slaves. The Civil War had begun in April 1861, after seven Southern states had broken away from the Union to form their own country, the Confederate States of America. Four more states soon joined them. President Abraham Lincoln argued that these states didn't have a legal right to separate from the United States. He fought the South to keep the Union whole. As the conflict went on, Lincoln made the Civil War a battle to end slavery across the United States.

Yet when Carver was born, slavery was still a

George Washington Carver posed for an early studio photograph.

way of life for 4 million African-Americans. Carver's mother was a young black slave named Mary. In 1855, when she was just 13, Mary was sold to a Missouri farmer named Moses Carver. A German immigrant, Carver generally opposed slavery. But he and his wife Susan had no children and could not work their farm alone, so he decided to buy Mary from a neighbor. She settled in on the Carver's farm just outside the town of Diamond Grove (now called simply Diamond) in southwestern Missouri's Newton County. Over the years, Mary had several children, though only two sons are known to have reached adulthood: Jim, who was born in 1859, and George.

As an adult, George Washington Carver was always unclear about when he was born. At one time, he said he was born "about the close of the great Civil War." Another time he stated, "I was about two weeks old when the war closed." Since the Civil War ended on April 9, 1865, that would put his birthday in late March. Today, however, many historians accept July 12, 1864, as his birth date.

Young George never knew his father, a slave who lived on a neighboring farm. According to what George did know, his father died while bringing a wagonload of wood to town. Somehow he slipped under the wagon and was run over. George also never got to know his mother, because he and his brother Jim were separated from her soon after George was

Though a slave-owner himself, Moses Carver opposed slavery on principle.

born. Like most of George's early years, the details of the separation are hazy.

During the Civil War, Missouri was a border state—along with Delaware, Maryland, and Kentucky. Missouri allowed slavery but remained loyal to the Union. People across Missouri were divided in their loyalties. Some supported the Union, while others sided with the Confederacy. Even though he owned slaves, Moses Carver favored the Union cause. In the area where he lived, however, many people supported the South, and at times Confederate troops operated in the region. So did raiders and outlaws of all kinds, who took advantage of the war's chaos to rob local farmers. Several times during the Civil War, Moses Carver was the target of raiders looking for money.

Confederate soldiers helped themselves to homemade pies during a Civil War raid in 1863.

As the war was coming to an end, another group of raiders came. Moses hid George's brother Jim, but the raiders kidnapped baby George and his mother. A friend of the Carvers was able to track down the raiders. The Carvers were relieved to see the friend return with the baby, though as George later wrote, "At that time I was nearly dead with the whooping cough that I had caught on the way." Mary, however, did not return. She was either killed by the kidnappers or sold to new owners. Not long afterward, on January 11, 1865, Missouri's leaders ended slavery in the state.

Now orphans, George and Jim moved from the farm's slave quarters—where the boys had lived with their mother—into the main house, a simple one-room log cabin with one window and a fireplace. The Carvers raised the brothers as if they were their own children.

The whooping cough that George caught during his kidnapping was the first of many

In his writings, George Washington Carver briefly mentioned the raid that took him from Moses Carver's farm. George wrote that he and his mother were "ku klucked," referring to the group called the Ku Klux Klan. In reality, the KKK was not formed until 1866, after the kidnapping had taken place. But for several years after the Civil War, the Klan was a real threat to freed slaves in the South. The KKK believed in white supremacy—the idea that whites were better than blacks. Klan members did not want former slaves to vote or have other legal rights. Wearing long robes and masks, KKK members attacked and sometimes killed African-Americans.

Though President Lincoln issued the Emancipation Proclamation on January 1, 1863, many African-Americans in the United States remained enslaved. Lincoln's decree freed the slaves living in the Southern states that had joined the Confederacy; it did not apply to the slaves of whites in Missouri and other border states that remained in the Union but permitted slavery. The Emancipation Proclamation also did not apply to West Virginia and parts of the Confederacy that had come under Union military control during the war. Slavery did not end everywhere in the United States until the passing of the 13th Amendment to the Constitution, late in 1865.

childhood illnesses he suffered. By all accounts, he was a weak, sickly boy, especially compared to his larger, stronger brother. But George was not always confined to his bed—farm life demanded that everyone in the family do what they could to help. The Carvers rose with the sun and put in long days raising corn, wheat, and other grains. George helped out by putting corn seeds in the ground and giving water to the farm animals. Most of his chores, however, were indoors, where he helped Susan Carver take care of the house. George learned to cook, sew, and do many other jobs considered "women's work." Some of those skills, such as doing laundry, became useful when he was an adult and living on his own.

Farm life was not all hard work. Moses Carver knew how to play a fiddle and would entertain the family. George shared his adoptive father's love of music and later learned to play accordion and piano. Jim and George took time after their chores to go fishing, swimming, and running through the fields. The two African-American boys played with white children and were surrounded by white

George (left) posed with his brother, Jim, in an early photo.

adults—the Carvers and their relatives and their neighbors in Diamond Grove.

The Carvers and other adults noticed that George was deeply curious about everything around him, especially nature. He enjoyed taking long walks across the unplanted areas of the Carver farm where wild animals and plants lived. George collected samples of flowers and planted them in a garden that

Originally a one-room structure, Moses Carver's farmhouse was later rebuilt and enlarged.

he kept hidden near the house. As he later explained, "[I]t was considered foolishness in the neighborhood to waste time on flowers." Soon, however, his family and friends saw that he had a natural skill for raising plants, and neighbors brought him sickly specimens. George was so good at reviving the plants that he soon became known as the "plant doctor." He later wrote, "[P]lants from all over the county would be brought to me for treatment." Young George and his neighbors probably never imagined how his talent with plants would come to shape his life.

Chapter

3 In Search of Knowledge

The people of Newton County, Missouri, marveled at George's skills with plants, and they recognized he had a gift that few people in the region, white or black, shared. As an adult, George traced his talents to God. George deeply believed in God and thought that God had chosen him to do special things. Once as a boy, George wanted a pocketknife but could not afford to buy one, so he asked God to send him one. That night he had a dream in which he saw a knife sticking out of a partially eaten watermelon that was leaning against some cornstalks on the farm. When he awoke, he went to the spot he saw in his dream and found a partially eaten watermelon—with the same knife he had seen in his dream. George was convinced that this vision and others he had later in

In George Washington Carver's time, schools were segregated. If an African-American wanted to receive an education, he or she attended a school for black children.

life came from God.

Moses Carver was not religious; George found religion on his own. When he was about 10 years old, "God just came into my heart one afternoon while I was alone in the loft of our big barn." He and Jim went to the local white church, where they heard ministers from different faiths. George never considered himself tied to the teachings of any one church. He was a mystic—someone who believed he could have direct contact with God through prayer and nature.

Although the Carvers didn't shape George's religious beliefs and practices, they did encourage him to get an education. Moses and Susan were not well educated, but they taught George the basics of reading and writing. George had one book in the house—*Webster's Elementary Spelling Book*. For a time, he took classes with white students at the local church, but some local residents opposed blacks and whites being in the same school, and at the time it was also against the law. George finally got the chance for a real education in about 1877, when the Carvers let him go to Neosho, seat of the government for Newton County.

Wearing his best clothes, George walked eight miles (12.8 kilometers) to Neosho. After he arrived, tired from his journey, he fell asleep in an open barn. The barn belonged to Mariah and Andrew Watkins,

George wrote on a slate as an elementary student in Neosho.

an African-American couple. Mariah was a midwife skilled in using herbs to cure the sick, and her husband did odd jobs around town. Mariah agreed to let George live with them. In exchange, he would do chores around the house. Andrew and Mariah Watkins became second "adoptive" parents for George and the first African-American adults he ever knew and loved.

Until this time, George was known as "Carver's George." Most slaves had been identified as their owner's property. Now George became known as

Though many Southerners opposed helping blacks, Missouri was one of the few former slave states that tried to educate blacks after the end of the Civil War. Its constitution called for free public education for both black and white students. Blacks were given their own schools if a township had more than 20 black students. In some townships with a small black population, the children were allowed to go to white schools. But even when black students had their own schools, finding skilled teachers was hard, as George Washington Carver learned in Neosho.

"George Carver." Later, he would choose *W* as a middle initial. When asked if it stood for "Washington," Carver said yes, giving him his full name so famous today.

In Neosho, George attended a school for blacks called the Lincoln School. The 75 students crowded into its one room to study with a young African-American man named Stephan Frost. George quickly came to believe he knew as much as, if not more than, his teacher. He decided to move on and look for a better school. The chance soon came, when he learned that a Neosho family was heading west to Kansas. There, George hoped, he could receive the education he craved. He agreed to take care of the family's mules in exchange for making the journey with them.

Kansas seemed like an attractive place for African-Americans to settle. It entered the Union as a free state in 1861, and some of its first settlers opposed slavery. John Brown, the famous abolitionist, fought pro-slavery forces in Kansas during the 1850s. Kansas had plenty of land,

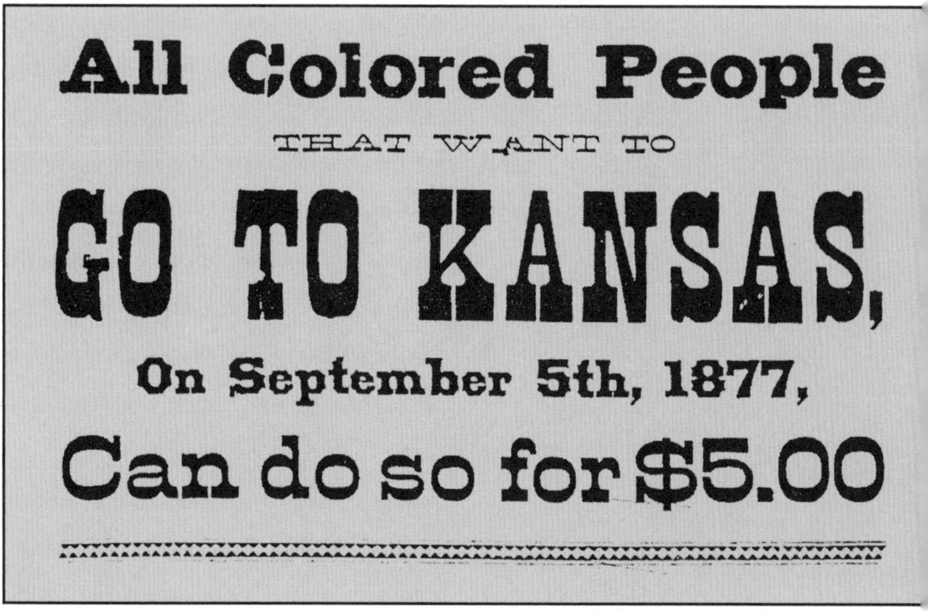
All Colored People
THAT WANT TO
GO TO KANSAS,
On September 5th, 1877,
Can do so for $5.00

An 1877 handbill urged African-Americans to settle in Kansas.

and former slaves hoping to escape the prejudice of the South flocked to the state. Between 1870 and 1880, the African-American population increased from 17,000 to 43,000.

Before George Washington Carver joined the black settlers going to Kansas, he went back to Diamond Grove. He said goodbye to the Carvers and to Jim, and then packed up his few belongings and headed west. The family George traveled with was going to Fort Scott, about 75 miles (120 kilometers) from Neosho.

When he reached Fort Scott, George looked for a job and a place to live. He worked as a cook for a while and saved up enough money to rent a tiny apartment. He took classes at the local school, often studying by candlelight late into the night. For a time, he lived with and worked for Felix Payne, a local African-American blacksmith. The Payne family let George stay in their house. In return, he cooked and did other household chores. He would later say, "I found employment just as a girl [would]." Soon, however, a sickening event led George to leave Fort Scott.

Before the Civil War, Fort Scott was in the middle of a region that was in conflict over the issue of slavery. Congress had created the territories of Kansas and Nebraska in 1854 and said their residents could decide whether or not to allow slavery. Slave owners from Missouri and other Southern states soon came to Kansas, hoping they could create another slave state. To counteract this effort, those who opposed slavery also came to Kansas. By 1856, the territory was known as "Bleeding Kansas" because of the violence between these rival groups.

Although Kansas had never allowed slavery, many white residents still had racist attitudes toward blacks. These people were quick to capture and abuse any black suspected of a crime. In 1879, a young black man from Fort Scott was accused of attacking a white girl. A group of masked white men tracked down the suspect and brought him to the center of town. Instead of turning him over to the police and giving him his day in court, the white men killed the black man. After dragging his body through the streets, the men threw the suspect's body onto a fire.

While living in Fort Scott, George found work doing household chores.

Soon afterward, George left town. Toward the end of his life, he remembered this disgusting incident. He said, "As young as I was, the horror haunted me and does even now." What he saw, however, never kept him from finding the good in people, both black and white.

Chapter

4 Years of Wandering

Still eager to pursue an education, George Washington Carver left Fort Scott and went to Olathe, Kansas. He moved in with Lucy and Ben Seymour, another African-American couple. When not attending school, George helped Mrs. Seymour with her laundry business and did other odd jobs around town. The Seymour family decided to leave Olathe, and for a time George lived with another family in nearby Paola. Then in 1880, he caught up with the Seymours in Minneapolis, Kansas, and he stayed there for several years.

During his time in Minneapolis, Carver went to high school. His classes included Latin and Greek. He impressed the other students and the teacher with his knowledge, and he received a gold pin in honor of his skills. Outside of class, Carver continued to

Between 1880 and 1890, George Washington Carver lived in eight different cities and held at least as many jobs.

do odd jobs, sometimes studying while he ironed or washed clothes.

When he was around 19, George returned to Diamond Grove to visit the Carvers and his brother, Jim. Because George had not grown much, he was able to pay a child's fare for the train. "The conductor," he later wrote, "thought I was rather small to be traveling alone." Some time after that, however, George shot up in height, reaching 6 feet (1.8 meters). But his voice remained quite high. People were sometimes startled to hear what sounded like a woman's voice

Carver attended high school (back left) in Minneapolis, Kansas.

coming from such a large body.

In 1884, back in Minneapolis, George learned that his brother had died not long after his visit. Though the loss made him feel all alone in the world, he later wrote, "I trusted God and pushed ahead." By the end of the year, he was in Kansas City, Missouri. George bought a typewriter and took courses at a local business school before landing an office job. The urge to continue his education, however, outweighed the desire to work. George applied to a small college in Highland, Kansas, and was soon accepted.

By this time in his life, George Washington Carver had often faced racism, but the attitudes of some whites at Highland College were especially damaging. Arriving in September 1885, he met the school's principal. The man looked at Carver and said, "There has been a mistake. You didn't tell me you were Negro. Highland College does not take Negroes." Years later, when writing about this time in his life, Carver merely said he "was refused on account of my color." Disheartened, he didn't bother to apply to another school.

Some local white families heard about Carver's troubles at Highland College. They tried to help him by giving him work. Carver became friends with the Beeler family. Mrs. Beeler hired him to do laundry and other chores. Carver also did laundry for some of the students at the college. After a year, Carver

Though he was admitted, Carver was not allowed to attend Highland College because of his race.

decided to leave town. One of the Beelers' children, Frank, had gone to Ness County in western Kansas and opened a store on the prairie. A small town called Beeler was developing around the land Frank settled. In the summer of 1886, Carver arrived in Ness County and claimed some land for himself.

For a time, Carver lived with and worked for George Steeley, a white rancher. He took the money he made on Steeley's ranch and bought seeds and tools for his own farm. Using just his own muscle, Carver planted 17 acres (6.8 hectares) of crops, including rice, corn, and vegetables. He also planted fruit trees and shrubs. By the spring of 1887, Carver had built a tiny sod house on his land.

In 1862, Congress had passed the Homestead Act to attract settlers to public lands in the Midwest. Americans desiring to own their own farms could claim 160 acres (64 hectares). If they lived on the land for five years, they received it for free, after paying a small fee. If the settlers did not want to wait five years, they could buy the land for $1.25 per acre. Settlers could also sell their claim to the land. Carver bought one of these claims from another settler.

Once again, Carver was living in a mostly white community. As usual, he had no trouble making friends. His wide range of talents impressed the people of Ness County. He had bought an accordion during his travels across Kansas, and he played it at local dances. He also joined a club that held weekly meetings to discuss current issues and the arts. And plants remained an important part of his life. On the Steeley ranch, Carver built a greenhouse, where he raised about 500 plants.

In Beeler, Kansas, Carver began pursuing a new interest—painting. Since boyhood, he had enjoyed sketching. Now he took art lessons from Clara Duncan, who had been a teacher at Talladega, one of the first African-American colleges in the South.

A group of musicians gathered outside a sod hotel in Beeler, Kansas, in the 1880s.

Duncan helped Carver draw and paint. She also schooled him in writing. Carver showed her a long poem that reflected some of his deepest beliefs. A portion of it read:

O! Sit not down nor idly stand;
There's plenty to do on every hand.
If you cannot prosper in work like some,
You've at least one talent, improve that one.

Duncan suggested that Carver focus on improving his general writing skills rather than trying to write poetry, and Carver took her advice. Painting, not poetry, became his main outlet for his artistic urges.

But painting was only a hobby, and other work took up most of Carver's time. Farm life was hard on the Kansas plains. Water was often in short supply. Carver tried to dig wells on his land but never hit water, and rain was scarce, making it hard to grow crops. Then, in the winter of 1888, a killer blizzard cut across the state. By that summer, Carver was ready to move on. He borrowed money from a local bank and set off for Iowa. Carver never farmed his homestead again, and he finally turned the land over to the bank in 1891. Yet later in life, he had fond memories of his time in Ness County. In 1935, he wrote to a former resident, "I do not recall a single instance in which I was not given an opportunity to develop the best that was within me."

The house that George Washington Carver built on his Kansas land was made of sod—blocks of grass with thick roots. These sod houses, or "soddies," were common shelters on the Plains, where wood was scarce. Settlers cut sod out of the ground and stacked it with the grass facing down, so it would not keep growing. A typical sod house was one story tall and had walls about 3 feet (.91 meters) thick. It could last five or six years, and even longer if the sod bricks were covered with paint or stucco, a mixture of cement and sand. For his house, Carver put in a wooden door and a small window. The roof had a wooden frame covered with tar paper and sod.

Carver settled in the town of Winterset, Iowa. He worked as head cook at the St. Nicholas Hotel and set up his own laundry business. Around 1890, a decision to visit a white church in Winterset changed his life.

Carver enjoyed singing in church, and his voice must have been easy to detect.

In his early years, Carver lived in many cities throughout the Midwest.

The day after the church service, a white man named Dr. John Milholland visited Carver at the hotel and said that his wife, Helen, wanted to meet him. Carver went with the doctor to the Milholland home and realized Mrs. Milholland was the lead singer in the church choir. Carver was astonished when she told him that his fine singing voice had attracted her attention. He began to study singing with her, and she took painting lessons from him. In the process, both Milhollands became close friends with Carver.

The Milhollands soon realized the range of Carver's talents and his intelligence. They urged him to think about going to college to pursue art and music. Carver decided to apply to Simpson College in nearby Indianola, Iowa. This time, he was sure to tell school officials that he was black. Carver did not have a high school diploma, but Simpson accepted him anyway. On September 9, 1890, Carver entered Simpson College, his next big step on his quest for knowledge.

Chapter

5 Success in College

The first days at Simpson College were not easy for George Washington Carver. Although the color of his skin was not a problem, his finances were. After paying the school fees, he had only a few cents left. He spent a dime on some corn and a nickel on some beef fat. While other male students rented rooms in private homes, Carver lived in an unused shack on the edge of campus. There he started a laundry business to raise money. He used credit to buy tubs, a washboard, and soap. The president of Simpson College promised Carver that he would tell students to bring their laundry to him. The president, however, forgot to mention the laundry business, and after a week, Carver was almost out of food. The president finally made his announcement, and Carver was in

In an early photograph, George Washington Carver posed with the painting he took to the World's Columbian Exposition.

business. "After that week," he later wrote, "I had many friends and plenty of work."

To furnish his new home, Carver collected wooden boxes from store owners and turned them into furniture. His stove came from a dump. As other students got to know and like Carver, they decided to help him. They knew he would not willingly take charity, so they went to work when he was out. One day when Carver returned home, he found that the students had "clubbed together and bought me a whole set of furniture—chairs, table, bed, and such things as I needed."

Carver also made friends among the townspeople and his teachers. Mrs. A.W. Liston, wife of a local bookstore owner, often invited Carver to her home and considered him part of the family. At Simpson College, Carver's most important influence was Etta

Carver spent a year studying art and botany at Simpson College in Indianola, Iowa.

Budd, an art teacher. At first, Budd did not think it was practical for an African-American to study art. She thought Carver needed to pursue studies that would help him get a job. But after she saw his skills, she let him take her classes. She noticed the way he painted flowers. Instead of copying from a model, he relied on his memory of the plants he had seen.

Still, Budd thought Carver should focus on a practical skill. She convinced him to give up art and study agricultural science at Iowa State College, one of the top agricultural schools in the United States. Budd's father was a professor there.

At first, Carver resisted her suggestion. Art was his true love. But he began to realize that she was right. He could find a good job if he had a degree in agricultural science. He could also use those skills to help other African-Americans who lacked his

intelligence or the chance for formal education. Later in life, Carver was grateful that he had taken Budd's advice. He wrote that he was "greatly indebted [to her] for whatever measure of success has come to me."

In May 1891, Carver arrived at the Iowa State campus in Ames. He was the only African-American student at the school, and he immediately experienced prejudice. Going into the dining hall, he was told he could not eat with white students. Instead, he had to go to the basement, where the school's black workers ate. Carver also heard students shout racist taunts

At Iowa State College, Carver (back row, second from right) stood out among his white fellow students.

his way. Carver wrote a letter to his friend Mrs. Liston of Indianola, and she came to Ames to help him adjust to his new surroundings. "The next day," Liston wrote, "everything was different ... and from then on, things went very much easier."

At Iowa State, Carver took a wide range of classes. History and math were his least favorite, while he did best in botany—the study of plants. Everyone at the school soon agreed that he was the best botany student at Iowa State. Carver formed close relationships with some of his teachers, including James Wilson and Louis Pammel. Wilson had come to the college to run its agricultural station, where farm experiments were done. Pammel, a professor of botany, helped Carver find a job as a school janitor.

Carver once again found it easy to make friends. He joined the college's National Guard unit and represented Iowa State at a

Iowa State College was one of many public colleges and universities in the United States that opened agricultural experiment stations. An 1887 law had set aside money to "aid in acquiring and diffusing [spreading] among the people of the United States useful and practical information on subjects connected with agriculture, and to promote scientific investigation and experiment respecting the principles and applications of agricultural science." Each station was instructed to release bulletins that would help farmers learn about the research being done. Later in his career, George Washington Carver helped Tuskegee Institute in Tuskegee, Alabama, acquire an agricultural station, which he led for many years.

At Iowa State College, Carver achieved the highest rank in the National Guard Student Battalion.

national conference for college students two years in a row. He also continued to paint, and in 1893 he received a great honor. One of his works was chosen to represent Iowa in an art show at the World's Columbian Exposition in Chicago, Illinois. The fair marked the 400th anniversary of the first voyage of Christopher Columbus to the Americas and attracted visitors from all over the world. Carver was lucky enough to attend as well, and his painting won an honorable mention.

At Iowa State, religion became an important part of Carver's life. He joined the Young Men's Christian Association (YMCA) and with Professor Wilson ran a religious study group. In a letter to the Milhollands in 1884, Carver wrote that he was "praying a great deal. I believe more and more in prayer all the time." His letters reflected his belief that God had chosen him to do great things with his life.

In 1894, Carver received his degree in agricultural science. When a local florist offered him a job, he said, "I did not earn my education in order to arrange flowers for the dead." Iowa State offered him a job as a botanist at the agricultural station, and he took that instead. At the same time, he pursued postgraduate studies.

At the agricultural station, Carver worked with crossbreeding. He also studied with Pammel, who was an expert in mycology—the study of fungi. This kingdom of organisms is made up of living matter that draw their nutrients from other living things, such

George Washington Carver bred his plants through a process called crossbreeding or cross-fertilization. In cross-fertilization, scientists seek to create plants with certain traits, such as a particular color or height. Pollen from a male plant with the desired trait is placed in a female plant with the desired trait. The seeds that the female plant produces are then grown and produce more plants with the desired trait. The plants created through this process are called hybrids. The branch of science that studies how one generation of plants or animals pass traits to the next is called genetics. The science of genetics was still new when Carver was in college. Today, genetic research allows scientists to easily create plants that resist insects or dry weather.

as plants. Mushrooms, yeasts, and molds are fungi. As in other areas, Carver seemed to have a natural talent for mycology. He could easily find fungi growing in the wild, and he became knowledgeable about certain fungi that caused disease in plants. During his postgraduate work, Carver helped write several scientific articles and collected samples of about 1,500 plants and fungi. His collection eventually grew to contain about 20,000 specimens. Pammel called Carver "a brilliant student, the best collector and the best scientific observer I have ever known."

Carver received his master's degree from Iowa State College in 1896, but even before then he was thinking about his future. Iowa State hoped he would stay in Ames to teach and do research. Alcorn Agricultural and Mechanical College, a school for African-Americans in Mississippi, wanted him to teach there. But early in 1896, he received an

invitation to teach at another black school in the South. The offer proved too good to pass up—and accepting it changed Carver's life.

Louis Pammel was a friend and mentor to Carver well beyond Carver's time at Iowa State College.

Chapter

6 Principal Washington and Professor Carver

In March 1896, George Washington Carver went on a speaking tour, drawing on his increasing knowledge of agriculture. When he returned to Ames, a letter was waiting for him from Booker T. Washington, principal of Tuskegee Institute in Tuskegee, Alabama. Washington was trying to make Tuskegee the best school for African-Americans in the country. Carver knew about Washington, who had gained fame for his call to blacks to "accommodate" themselves to life in the South. Rather than protest their treatment, Washington thought blacks should educate themselves, start successful businesses, and become independent in economic matters. In this way, they would prove their worth to white society. Then, Washington believed, racism and prejudice would

Booker T. Washington founded Tuskegee Institute in Tuskegee, Alabama, in 1881.

Like George Washington Carver, Booker Taliaferro Washington (1856–1915) was born a slave. And like Carver, Washington hungered for education. After he won his freedom, Washington taught himself to read with Webster's Elementary Spelling Book, *the same book Carver first read as a child. Washington went on to study at Virginia's Hampton Institute. In 1881, he opened Tuskegee Institute. Like Carver, he believed in the value of hard work and told students at Tuskegee, "Nothing ever comes to one, that is worth having, except as a result of hard work." In 1901, Washington published his autobiography,* Up from Slavery, *which quickly became a best seller.*

begin to fade. On the whole, Carver agreed with these goals.

By 1896, Washington had also heard of Carver, who was about to become the only black man in America with an advanced degree in agricultural science. Tuskegee was ready to open a department of agriculture, and Washington wanted Carver to run it. Carver was not sure what to do. He still had work to do on his master's degree, and he already had the offer from Alcorn. In his reply to Washington, Carver did not take the job, but he indicated he might be open to it.

Two days later, Carver contacted Washington again. He wrote that if he got a satisfactory position, he might be convinced to leave before getting his degree. The two men exchanged several more letters, and by mid-May Carver had a new job. He would also have time to finish his degree. Carver wrote:

I am looking forward to a very busy, pleasant and profitable time at your college and shall be glad to cooperate with you in doing all I can through Christ who strengtheneth me to better the condition of our people.

In October 1896, Carver left Ames for Tuskegee, Alabama. He brought with him his master's degree, a new microscope from his friends, and the certainty that he was doing God's work. For the first time in his life, Carver would be living in the Deep South.

Tuskegee students helped build the institute's campus.

In 1896, the same year Carver joined the staff at Tuskegee Institute, the Supreme Court heard an important legal case that had a long-lasting impact on blacks. An African-American named Homer Plessy challenged the segregation of whites and blacks on Louisiana trains. The court ruled in Plessy v. Ferguson *that segregation was legal as long as the separate services for blacks were equal to the ones offered whites. Though in reality black schools, hospitals, and other services were not as good, segregation remained the law of the land for the rest of Carver's life. It wasn't until 1954 that Jim Crow laws were struck down with the Supreme Court's ruling in* Brown v. Board of Education.

Alabama was a former Confederate state that had been dominated by cotton plantations worked by slaves. African-Americans outnumbered whites in many areas, yet even with the end of slavery, whites controlled the state's politics and economy.

Washington wanted Tuskegee Institute to give African-Americans hope for a better future. The school taught students from elementary school to high school, and adults came to learn skills such as carpentry, brick making, and printing. Among the teachers at Tuskegee, Carver stuck out in several ways. Few of the others had gone to white colleges, and none of them held a master's degree from a white school. Carver was darker-skinned than some of the teachers, and even African-Americans judged others by the color of their skin. His personal habits struck some people as odd. He knitted his own scarves, wore old clothes, and didn't socialize much with other teachers. He focused on teaching and investigating

Students at Tuskegee Institute learned practical skills such as printing.

the plants he found all around him.

On his walks, Carver sometimes carried a box to collect plant specimens. One day, a white woman saw him and stopped to talk. When she learned about his skill with plants, she asked him to look at some of her diseased roses. He showed her what to do to help them recover. Word quickly spread around Tuskegee, and "people began calling upon me for information and advice." Once again, the "plant doctor" was open for business. And once again, George Washington Carver made white friends because of his talents and desire to help others.

Yet not everything went smoothly at Tuskegee. To some of the other teachers, Carver seemed arrogant. When he arrived at the school, he asked for two rooms. At the time, two unmarried male teachers had to share a room because of lack of space. Carver wrote a letter to school officials, complaining that he needed a room for his equipment and specimens. He eventually got the space in one of the buildings that housed male students. In the same letter, he talked about his desire to stay at Tuskegee just a few years and then "engage in my brush work"—his beloved painting. Other teachers heard this and thought Carver was not committed to his work at Tuskegee.

Throughout his career at Tuskegee Institute, George Washington Carver remained single. He had a close relationship with Sarah L. Hunt, a relative of a Tuskegee official, and at one point considered marrying her. He wrote his friend Mrs. Liston for advice, but in the end, Carver decided that he and Hunt were not right for each other. Instead, he devoted himself to his studies, his religion, and the young people he met at Tuskegee and in his travels around the country.

Carver, however, filled his days with hard work trying to build the new agricultural department. When he began teaching in October 1896, he had 13 students. By the end of the school year, he had 76 students and had created a two-year plan of study for the department. With five assistants, Carver took care of the school's dairy, livestock, and vegetables. At times, he acted as the school's veterinarian. He also ran a small weather station, sending information on rainfall and temperature to scientists in Montgomery, Alabama's capital.

Soon after he arrived at Tuskegee, the school received money to open an agricultural experiment station. It was the first station operated by a black school. Carver took control of that as well and

At Tuskegee, Carver (standing, back right, with faculty) was no longer the only African-American.

published the first of several dozen bulletins for farmers in 1898. Its subject: feeding acorns to hogs.

Although Washington appreciated Carver's skills, he did not always agree with the scientist. Washington was a practical man with practical concerns—such as raising money for the entire school. Carver did not care about the day-to-day tasks of running a department. He wanted to do research and explore new ideas. To do this, he sought to improve conditions at the agricultural station. He wrote several letters to Washington begging for help. In one from 1898,

Carver (second from right) was most interested in working with students and doing agricultural research.

Carver wrote:

> *Here I am working with the smallest and most inexperienced staff of any station in the U.S. ... It is impossible for me to do this work without men and means.*

Washington, however, largely ignored Carver's plea, which upset the professor even more. Four years later, he was still complaining that his work was being compromised because of the school's demands on him. At times, Carver disliked some of his duties, which included taking care of the school's farm and its chickens.

Washington sometimes had mixed feelings about Carver. The founder of Tuskegee called Carver "a great teacher, a great lecturer, a great inspirer of young men and old men." Yet he also said that Carver had no ability to do practical farm work. His true skills, Washington said—and Carver also knew—were in "inspiring and instructing young men after they are secured and placed before him in a class" and in his "unusual ability in the direction of original research." At Tuskegee, Carver developed both of those skills.

Chapter 7 Life in the Lab and the Classroom

Raising chickens and running a farm was not why George Washington Carver had come to Tuskegee. He wanted to help black farmers raise more crops and improve their lives. That was the goal of his work at the experiment station. He wrote in 1904:

> *The experiment station ... is devoted to all kinds of experiments with a view to increasing the quantity and quality of our farm crops, by fertilizer experiments, test of varieties, cross-breeding of plants, the testing of new varieties etc.*

Carver did not have his own laboratory at Tuskegee, and he was not a chemist. But he had enough skills to analyze water and soils and to create

Carver's work at Tuskegee Institute was aimed at helping farmers learn to grow a variety of crops.

new products from natural resources. Carver built a small lab for himself, as he put it, out of "bottles, old fruit jars, and any other things I found I could use." With these items, along with teacups and glasses, he carried out experiments on his writing desk. After 1910, when he was named director of agricultural research at Tuskegee, Carver finally had a real lab, although it was small.

To Carver, the major problem for Alabama farmers was their reliance on one main crop, cotton. If cotton prices fell or the crop was hurt by drought, farmers faced tough economic times. Cotton also took nutrients out of the soil faster than other crops. Carver believed that Southern farmers needed to

Carver's first laboratory is now on display at Tuskegee's George Washington Carver Museum.

grow other crops besides cotton, or at least rotate cotton with crops less harmful to the soil.

One of the first crops Carver suggested that farmers raise was the cowpea. This legume added nitrogen to the soil. Using legumes to strengthen the soil was cheaper than buying chemical fertilizer. Carver believed that keeping the soil rich through natural means led to healthier crops.

To show that the cowpea was more than just a soil nutrient, Carver used it to create a variety of foods. In one of his early bulletins from the agricultural experiment station, he wrote that the cowpea provided "food for both man and beast." He included recipes for making soup, pudding, salads, and pancakes from cowpeas.

The next crop Carver focused on was the sweet potato. The root vegetable was easy to grow, and farmers could plant and harvest the crop twice in one year. Sweet potatoes also stayed fresh a long

During the 19th century, cotton earned its nickname, "King Cotton," as the main crop throughout much of the South. The invention of the cotton gin in 1793 prompted Southern farmers to plant more cotton. They also began buying more slaves to grow and pick the cotton. The huge increase in the number of slaves owned in the South was tied to the rising production of cotton. After slavery ended, many freed blacks raised cotton as sharecroppers, renting their land from wealthy whites and giving them a share of their cotton as payment. Often, the sharecroppers could not produce enough cotton to pay their debts. Carver believed the poor farmers needed to grow a variety of crops to have a better chance of escaping debt.

time, and Carver discovered they could last longer if they were dehydrated. He showed farmers how to dry them on a stove or in the sun on hot days. Then he roasted and ground them to use as a coffee. In years of experimenting with sweet potatoes, Carver created more than 100 products. These included

Carver showed farmers that the sweet potato was both versatile and easy to grow.

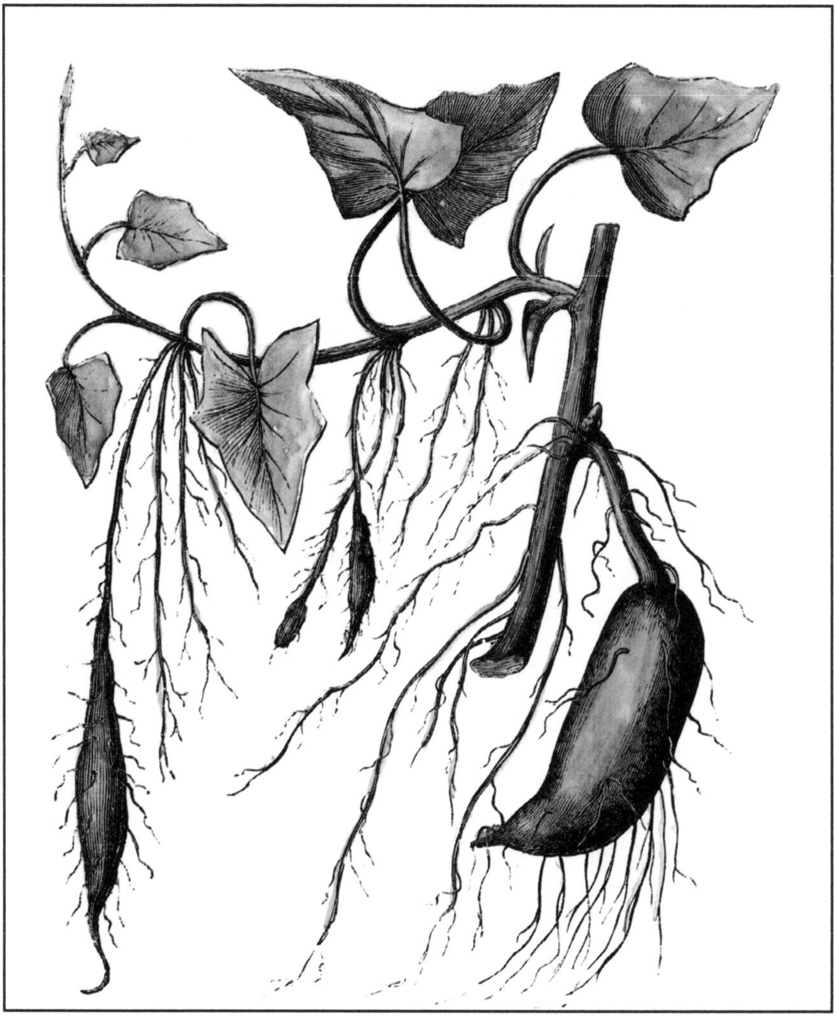

sweet potato flour and sugar, animal feed, and dyes and paints.

During the early 1900s, Carver saw a greater need for Southern farmers to turn away from cotton. By then, a destructive bug called the boll weevil was working its way through the South. The weevil ate the cotton before it could be picked. Carver thought that the peanut was a better crop to raise. It was easy to grow, added nitrogen to the soil, and would not be harmed by boll weevils. The peanut also provided a cheap source of protein for people who couldn't always afford to buy meat. In 1903, Carver began raising peanuts at the experiment station and working in his lab to find new uses for the plant. He also gathered recipes, which he later published in his bulletins.

Although Carver became most famous for his work with sweet potatoes and peanuts, he studied other crops as well. Booker T. Washington asked him to work with cotton. He also raised soybeans and alfalfa and created new hybrids of vegetables. He amazed local farmers when he grew huge crops on land that had been used as a dump. Using legumes and natural fertilizers to strengthen the soil, Carver grew cabbages that weighed 20 pounds (9 kilograms) and onions bigger than softballs.

Carver also tried to find ways to use wastes produced on farms and in factories. Sawdust could be mixed with glue and turned into material that looked like marble. Pine cones, peanut shells, and banana skins could be turned into wallboard for building homes. Peanut skins were part of a paper that he made, and the stalk of the okra plant became a fiber in rugs. Carver did most of his work alone, because the Tuskegee experiment station did not have enough staff and funding. The shortage forced him to develop skills in many areas of science, rather than specialize in botany, as he had once hoped he would do.

Plants were not the only subject of Carver's work. As he learned on nature walks around Tuskegee, Alabama soils contain many types of clay. Carver took samples back to his lab and began creating paints and stains from the clay. Still interested in painting, he used some of these paints for his own work. Other paints were used outdoors on buildings around Tuskegee. Carver was proudest of a rich blue color he created.

Not all of Carver's time was spent doing research. He was a teacher, and he loved the subjects he taught. He tried to stir the same love in his students. Nature, he believed, was the best teacher. He wrote in 1902, "The study of Nature is both entertaining and instructive ... it encourages investigation and stimulates originality."

Carver brought in plants and animals that he gathered in the wild, and he often took his students

Carver enjoyed bringing his students into the field to study nature.

outdoors. He also encouraged his students to collect specimens and share them with him. Once, a group of students tried to trick their teacher. They took parts from several different insects and assembled their own "bug." They asked Carver to identify it, as he had done with other specimens they had found. Carver quickly saw through the trick and called the insect a humbug.

In class, Carver expected his students to work hard. But outside, he enjoyed joking with them. At times, he loaned or gave students money and took an interest in their personal lives. He also shared with them his love of God, teaching a Bible class in his spare time. Up to 100 students crowded into a room to hear his thoughts on God, nature, and science. Carver's words and kind ways earned him the respect of many students. One former student wrote, "Pencil and paper can not express my thanks to you for your kindness and generous attention you gave me."

Carver's efforts to educate didn't end with his students. He had farmers come to the school so he could explain his work on improving the soil and show them the products he had made from plants. In 1892, Booker T. Washington held a conference for local farmers. Under Carver, the yearly Farmers' Conference grew bigger, with white and black farmers attending. He obtained packets of seeds from the U.S. government, which he gave to farmers, along with seeds for plants he grew at Tuskegee.

Carver also held monthly meetings called the Farmers' Institute to teach local farmers about new farming methods. Over time, he realized he could reach more farmers if he brought the classroom to them. In 1906, Washington and Carver worked together to create the Jesup Agricultural Wagon. Named for a wealthy white donor, the wagon traveled to nearby farms. The U.S. government liked the idea of a "movable school" and soon made the Jesup Agricultural Wagon part of the Department of Agriculture. James Wilson, Carver's professor from Iowa State, was the U.S. secretary of agriculture

during most of Carver's first two decades at Tuskegee. He tried to help Carver whenever he could and told others about his work. As the years went on, Carver won more praise for his efforts.

Originally a horse-drawn wagon, the Jesup Agricultural Wagon was later replaced by a truck.

Chapter 8 The Wizard of Tuskegee

As George Washington Carver traveled around the South speaking to farmers and other scientists, he was sometimes called the Wizard of Tuskegee. The name called to mind another great experimenter—Thomas A. Edison, who invented the phonograph and perfected the lightbulb. Edison was called the Wizard of Menlo Park. Edison, however, never taught school, and he didn't make deep, personal connections with people as Carver did. Edison was a businessman as well as a scientist. He held more than 1,000 patents and always looked for ways to develop products he could sell. Carver was less concerned about making money. He held three patents and never had much success with business. He was more interested in research and education. Carver wanted his work to

Carver's work in the lab led to numerous inventions—and great public acclaim.

benefit as many people as possible, especially the poor. "Sometimes," Carver once wrote, "money is the least thing we need."

The growing fame Carver won, however, did appeal to him. He knew he had great talents, and he liked it when others noticed them. At times, however, he thought people were too generous with their praise. Carver always said that whatever he did was the result of God's work.

Carver's Tuskegee laboratory was filled with his inventions.

In 1915, Booker T. Washington died. Although he and Carver had often disagreed, Carver deeply

respected the principal and was saddened by his death. One positive change, however, came after Washington's passing. The new principal of Tuskegee, Robert Russa Moton, highly respected Carver and let him do less teaching and more experimenting in the lab. Carver also began to travel even more to discuss his work.

Over two decades, George Washington Carver developed a good relationship with Robert Russa Moton (1867–1940). Like Booker T. Washington, Moton studied at the Hampton Institute. He then spent 25 years working at that school before coming to Tuskegee. Under Moton, Tuskegee added several new buildings and courses of study. For the first time, the institute offered college degrees. Carver praised Moton, saying, "You are making such valuable history for the race along so many lines."

Starting in 1916, more people began to realize Carver's talents and give him public praise. This acclaim began when he was asked to join the Royal Society of Arts in London that year. The group honored artists, scientists, and inventors of all kinds. A U.S. group called the National Agricultural Society also asked Carver to join. Soon newspapers were writing about Carver, focusing on his humble birth as a slave and his rise to greatness.

During this time, many of the nations in Europe were fighting World War I. The United States entered the war in 1917, and Carver's growing fame earned him an invitation to Washington, D.C. The war was leading to food shortages, which would grow worse as the

United States tried to feed several million troops and help its European allies. Government officials were eager to find substitutes for foods that were in short supply. In January 1918, Carver met with members of the Department of Agriculture. He showed them sweet potato flour, which he had developed years before. The officials were also interested in his work on dehydration, since it reduced the amount of fresh food that spoiled. The government did some experiments with drying potatoes through the rest of the war, which ended in November 1918.

By this time, the Wizard of Tuskegee was on his way to earning his new nickname—the Peanut Man. In 1916, he published a bulletin called *How to Grow the Peanut and 105 Ways of Preparing It for Human Consumption*. The bulletin reflected his long years of study on the legume. Carver often said that a "conversation" with God spurred his research. He told God that he wanted to know all about peanuts, and "the Creator told me to take them apart and resolve [separate] them into their elements." God instructed him to use pressure and temperature to combine the parts in different ways, he said, leading to many peanut products.

In 1919, Carver made perhaps his greatest peanut product, peanut milk. As word of the milk spread, Carver caught the attention of an Alabama peanut grower. Through him, Carver made his way

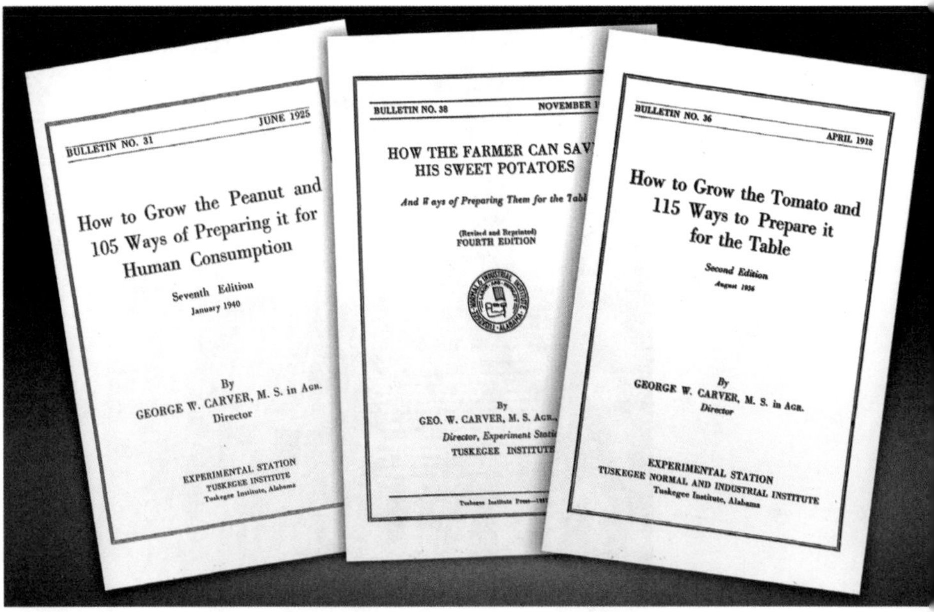

BULLETIN NO. 31
JUNE 1925
How to Grow the Peanut and 105 Ways of Preparing it for Human Consumption
Seventh Edition
January 1940
By
GEORGE W. CARVER, M. S. in Agr.
Director
EXPERIMENTAL STATION
TUSKEGEE INSTITUTE
BULLETIN NO. 38
HIS SWEET POTATOES
FOURTH EDITION
By
GEO. W. CARVER, M. S. Agr.
TUSKEGEE INSTITUTE
BULLETIN NO. 36
APRIL 1918
How to Grow the Tomato and 115 Ways to Prepare it for the Table
Second Edition
By
GEORGE W. CARVER, M. S. in Agr.
Director
EXPERIMENTAL STATION
TUSKEGEE NORMAL AND INDUSTRIAL INSTITUTE
Tuskegee Institute, Alabama

Carver reached out to farmers in simple, straightforward language with his many bulletins.

to the 1920 United Peanut Association meeting in Montgomery, where he made a strong impression on the peanut growers.

The next year, Carver's trip to Congress cemented his position as the Peanut Man. Once again, he packed up his samples of peanut products to show a committee made up of members of the U.S. House of Representatives. These lawmakers were considering whether or not to place a tariff on foreign peanuts. Carver didn't look like a highly respected scientist. He didn't like to spend money on clothes, and the suit he wore that day was nearly threadbare. But Carver's words were what mattered most.

The lawmakers gave Carver 10 minutes to speak.

Carver continued to collect plant specimens throughout his career, including one of a peanut plant.

But as he pulled more peanut products out of his bag, the members urged him to go on. At one point, he made the audience laugh when he said, "Here is a breakfast food. I am very sorry that you can not taste this, so I will taste it for you." Carver showed the lawmakers peanut flour, skins that could be used to make dyes, and peanut milk. When he was finally done, almost two hours had passed, and the lawmakers clapped their approval. Congress later passed the tariff.

In 1923, Carver won another honor for his work—the Spingarn Medal. This award was given each year by the National Association for the Advancement of Colored People (NAACP) to honor the work of an African-American. The NAACP said Carver earned the medal not only for his research, but also his lectures, "where his clear thought and straightforward attitude have greatly increased inter-racial knowledge and respect." Five years later, Simpson College gave Carver an honorary doctorate. People who are awarded that college degree are called doctors, and Carver often used that title.

The NAACP was founded in 1909 by several whites and blacks concerned about the legal rights of African-Americans. The most prominent African-American in the group was the scholar W.E.B. Du Bois (1868–1963). Du Bois and other members of the NAACP thought black people should fight for their political and legal rights and use them to win equality with whites. Du Bois also wrote about what he called the "talented tenth"—the 10 percent of the black population who needed a college education so they could lead other African-Americans to equality. Carver certainly belonged to this talented tenth.

During the 1920s, Carver also focused on his religious work. In 1923, he began a long relationship with the Commission on Interracial Cooperation (CIC). The commission wanted blacks and whites to understand each other better. The CIC often worked with the YMCA, a human-service organization,

Carver spoke at Simpson College, where he had been a student for a year and from which he received an honorary doctorate.

and the two groups asked Carver to speak at a conference held in Blue Ridge, North Carolina. There, in the audience, he spotted a young man named Jim Hardwick. After Carver spoke, he went up to Hardwick and said, "I want you to be one of my boys." Hardwick, the grandson of a former slave owner, didn't know what to think of this statement. Carver explained that he always chose some young men as his "adopted" sons, since he didn't have any children of his own. The professor tried to teach these young men to devote their lives to God and finding the truth.

Later, at home, Hardwick found himself thinking of Carver, "and instantly it seemed that his spirit filled the room. ... A peace entered me, and my problems fell away." Hardwick became the first of what Carver called his Blue Ridge Boys. Carver and these white boys wrote each other often, often about spiritual concerns. Hardwick and Carver wrote each other for more than 10 years, and Hardwick and other Blue Ridge Boys sometimes traveled with Carver when he gave lectures.

As the 1920s went on, Carver spent more time on the road. In 1925, he stopped doing fieldwork at the experiment station, though he still spent time in the lab. He also continued to promote peanuts, and he did some work for a peanut-processing company. The Tom Huston Company first contacted Carver in 1924, and the professor gave the company advice—free of charge—for years to come. He turned down a chance to work for Tom Huston, saying, "My work is a great publicity asset for the school [Tuskegee] and my race."

By the late 1920s, Carver's reputation had become forever tied to the peanut.

Helping others drove Carver in his efforts, not making money. Since he lived at Tuskegee and rarely spent money on himself, he saved most of his income.

Like many Americans, however, he lost most of his money when the Great Depression began. During the Depression, businesses closed and millions of Americans lost their jobs. By 1933, one out of four people couldn't find a job. As Americans rushed to take their money out of banks, many of the banks failed—including the one where Carver had his savings. He was upset that he wouldn't have money to help the poor in Tuskegee, not that he had lost the money.

The Great Depression, however, brought attention to Carver's work. His call for reducing waste and living simply appealed to poor farmers. The 1930s also saw Carver doing more work with his beloved peanut.

Chapter

9 Working till the End

During 1930, while assisting the Tom Huston Company, George Washington Carver noted some fungi that were harming peanut crops. He wrote a report on his findings, which was sent to peanut farmers across the South. Carver had never lost his interest in mycology, and some of his most important work during the 1930s would deal with fungi. In 1935, the U.S. government asked him to work with its mycology experts on plant diseases caused by fungi. Two years later, a type of tree fungi was named for him—*Taphrina carveri*. The mycology studies reflected some of Carver's best scientific work.

But it was the peanut, still, that brought him fame. Earlier that decade, one of Carver's peanut products was a face cream. He heard from some women who

Carver spent much of his 47-year career at Tuskegee doing hands-on work in his laboratory.

used the cream that it made their faces fat. Carver began to wonder if the peanut oil in the cream was the cause—and if so, if it could be put to good use. He decided to use the oil to massage the limbs of two children who had polio. In some cases, the disease left muscles withered and limbs paralyzed. Carver believed that the oil massages helped the children's muscles grow and their limbs gain strength.

Polio is a disease that attacks the body's nervous system. In severe cases, the limbs become paralyzed, and in the worst cases, the muscles that control breathing stop working and the patient dies. Polio was once common in the United States, and President Franklin D. Roosevelt lost the use of his legs because of the disease. During the early 1950s, Dr. Jonas Salk created a polio vaccine, which has been used by international health experts to almost completely wipe out the disease. Today, the number of people with polio is typically fewer than 1,000 per year worldwide.

In 1933, a reporter wrote about Carver and his work with polio patients. Carver said that he had not found a cure for polio, but his peanut-oil massages offered hope. The news article noted that "one of the subjects who had been walking with crutches was able to walk with the use of only a cane."

The story appeared around the country, and soon Carver was flooded with letters from adult polio victims and parents seeking help for their children. People suffering from polio came to Tuskegee, thinking he had a miracle cure. Carver was convinced that peanut oil somehow strengthened the muscles. People across the United States rushed out to buy peanut oil, creating a temporary shortage.

Carver treated patients for several years with good results. He also wrote to doctors and described his methods. Massaging the muscles was the key. At Iowa State, Carver had worked with some of the school's sports teams. He often massaged the athletes' aching muscles. With the polio patients, his massages and the hope he gave them—as well as exercises—

In the 1930s, Carver met U.S. President Franklin D. Roosevelt, himself a polio victim.

helped many of them improve. Carver, however, continued to say that peanut oil was an essential part of the treatment. In reality, it was the massage and exercise that seemed to do the most good for polio victims.

Since Carver didn't take money for his massage treatments, some grateful patients made donations to Tuskegee Institute. In 1939, the school received money from the National Foundation for Infantile Paralysis to open a clinic for young African-Americans with polio. Carver's friendship with Secretary of Agriculture Henry A. Wallace helped as well. Wallace was the son of one of Carver's professors at Iowa State, and the two men had been acquainted since Wallace was a boy. As secretary of agriculture, Wallace sent a letter to the foundation that suggested he was interested in Carver's work.

Wallace made several visits to Tuskegee during the 1930s. U.S. President Franklin D. Roosevelt also stopped by the school and met with Carver. But the professor's closest famous friend was the automaker Henry Ford. The two men shared an interest in what was called chemurgy—using crops to make industrial products. The word was first used in 1934, when Carver had already spent decades turning peanuts and other plants into useful products. He said, "[W]e can learn to synthesize materials for every human need from the things that grow."

Automaker Henry Ford (right) presented Carver with a modern, fully equipped laboratory for food research.

Ford hoped to use plastics made from soybeans in his cars. The plastic would be much lighter than steel. In 1937, Ford sponsored a chemurgical conference in Michigan. Carver spoke at the conference and met Ford for the first time. Each man respected the other's work, and Carver was thrilled to begin a friendship with him. Early in 1938, Carver wrote to Ford that he considered the automaker the greatest man he had ever met. Ford visited Carver at Tuskegee that same year. Two years later, Carver visited Ford's estate in Ways, Georgia. Ford had named a school there for Carver.

By this time, Carver's health was failing. When he felt strong enough, he took trips to speak and receive various honors. At times, he gave radio interviews, which brought his words to people across the country. Carver also put his energy into starting the George Washington Carver Museum at Tuskegee. He hoped the displays would inspire young people to pursue careers in science. He built a space for a lab, and the museum displayed some of the fungi and clays he had found during his long career. Henry Ford donated money to build the museum, and he was there when it opened in 1941.

Carver had always lived simply, and by 1940 he had saved $33,000, the equivalent of nearly $480,000 today. He used that money to start the George Washington Carver Foundation, which funded agricultural research at Tuskegee.

In 1942, Ford once again showed his appreciation for Carver. In Dearborn, Michigan, Ford built a village dedicated to U.S. history. He included a model of the cabin Carver lived in as a boy in Missouri. Carver went to the opening of the cabin and stayed several weeks in Michigan. That visit, however, was one of the last long trips Carver would take. By the start of 1943, Carver's health worsened, and on January 5, the great scientist died at the age of 78. He was buried at Tuskegee next to Booker T. Washington. That same year, the U.S. government honored Carver by calling for the George Washington Carver National Monument to be opened in Diamond, Missouri. His monument was the first in the United States to honor an African-American.

In the decades since Carver's death, scientists

A statue of Carver as a boy stands at the George Washington Carver National Monument.

Carver's gravestone acknowledges his achievements as a creative scientist.

and historians have debated his scientific work. Even during his lifetime, Carver had critics. In 1924, *The New York Times* attacked his statement, "No books ever go into my laboratory." The paper thought Carver put too much stress on God and not enough on serious scientific study. Carver did not leave detailed notes about his work. He tended to follow his intuition, rather than conduct scientific experiments that others could duplicate.

Henry A. Wallace, the former secretary of agriculture, believed that Carver was a great man. Yet he claimed that Carver's ability as a chemist had been somewhat overrated. A U.S. government study of Carver's work had a similar view. But in recent years, some historians have argued that Carver did indeed do many great things. Through his work, Carver helped many poor farmers improve their lives. He also talked about issues that are still important today: improving soil without chemicals, using plants in industry to replace fuels and minerals, and trying to save natural resources. Carver was an intelligent man with a strong curiosity about many subjects. He was more concerned with solving problems than doing original research.

In fact, George Washington Carver's greatest work may have happened outside of the lab. He inspired African-Americans to seek education and work hard, and he convinced white people that African-Americans could help society. He brought together members of both races and helped them understand each other. He also taught people to see the wonders of nature. Carver was a great example of a person dedicated to helping others in everything he did.

Life and Times

Carver's Life

1864
Born July 12 in Diamond Grove, Missouri

1880
Settles in Minneapolis, Kansas, where he attends high school

1885
Is prevented from entering Highland College because of his race

1865

1865
Slavery is abolished in the United States

1881
Booker T. Washington founds Tuskegee Institute

1886
Grover Cleveland dedicates the Statue of Liberty in New York Harbor, a gift from the people of France

World Events

1890

Enters Simpson College in Iowa

1891

Transfers to Iowa State College

1894

Earns a degree in agricultural science and begins working at Iowa State College

1890

1889

The Eiffel Tower opens in Paris, France

1893

Women gain voting privileges in New Zealand, the first country to take such a step

Life and Times

Carver's Life

1896
Earns a master's degree in agricultural science; begins teaching at Tuskegee Institute

1897
Becomes director of the agricultural experiment station at Tuskegee

1903
Begins raising peanuts at the experiment station

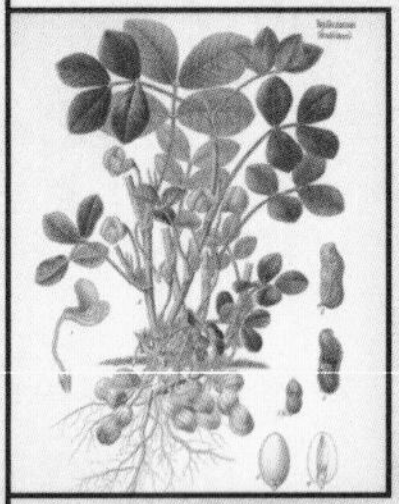

1900

1896
The first modern Olympic Games are held in Athens, Greece

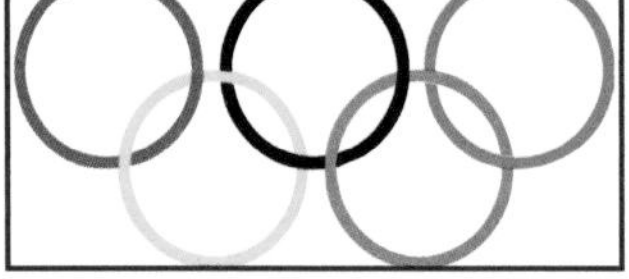

1898
The Spanish-American War gains Cuba its independence; Spain cedes the Philippines, Guam, and Puerto Rico to the United States for $20 million

1903
Brothers Orville and Wilbur Wright successfully fly a powered airplane

World Events

1906

Helps develop the Jesup Agricultural Wagon, a "movable school," to educate farmers

1916

Receives invitation to join the Royal Society of Arts and the National Agricultural Society

1920

Speaks to the United Peanut Association of America

1910

1906

Earthquake and fires destroy most of San Francisco; more than 3,000 people die

1916

German-born physicist Albert Einstein publishes his general theory of relativity

1920

American women get the right to vote

Carver's Life

1921
Appears before Congress to promote peanuts

1923
Receives the Spingarn Medal from the NAACP; attends his first conference for the Commission on Interracial Cooperation in Blue Ridge, North Carolina

1933
Wins attention for his treatment of polio victims

1930

1923
Irish civil war ends and the rebels sign a peace treaty

1933
Nazi leader Adolf Hitler is named chancellor of Germany

World Events

1935

Begins studies of fungi for the U.S. Department of Agriculture

1941

George Washington Carver Museum opens at Tuskegee

1943

Dies January 5 at Tuskegee Institute

1945

1935

Persia is renamed Iran

1941

Japanese bombers attack Pearl Harbor, Hawaii, on December 7, and the United States enters World War II

1943

U.S. General Dwight D. Eisenhower becomes the supreme Allied commander

Life at a Glance

Date of Birth:	July 12, 1864
Birthplace:	Diamond Grove, Missouri
Father:	Unknown
Mother:	Mary Carver (1842–?)
Education:	Bachelor's and master's degrees from Iowa State College, Ames, Iowa
Date of Death:	January 5, 1943
Place of Burial:	Tuskegee, Alabama

Further Reading

Federer, William J. *George Washington Carver: His Life & Faith in His Own Words*. St. Louis: Amerisearch, Inc., 2002.

Miller, Raymond H. *George Washington Carver*. Farmington Hills, Mich.: Kidhaven Press, 2005.

Rennert, Richard, ed. *Pioneers of Discovery*. New York: Chelsea House, 1994.

Wilson, Camilla. *George Washington Carver: The Genius Behind the Peanut*. New York: Scholastic, 2003.

Look for more Signature Lives books about this era:

Clara Barton: *Founder of the American Red Cross*

Amelia Earhart: *Legendary Aviator*

Thomas Alva Edison: *Great American Inventor*

Yo-Yo Ma: *Internationally Acclaimed Cellist*

Thurgood Marshall: *Civil Rights Lawyer and Supreme Court Justice*

Annie Oakley: *American Sharpshooter*

Will Rogers: *Cowboy, Comedian, and Commentator*

Amy Tan: *Writer and Storyteller*

Madam C.J. Walker: *Entrepreneur and Millionaire*

Booker T. Washington: *Innovative Educator*

On the Web

For more information on this topic, use FactHound.

1. Go to *www.facthound.com*
2. Type in this book ID: 0756518822
3. Click on the *Fetch It* button.

FactHound will find the best Web sites for you.

Historic Sites

George Washington Carver National Monument
5646 Carver Road
Diamond, MO 64840
417/325-4151

Carver's birthplace site, now a national monument, with a museum, nature trail, and replica of the Carver cabin

George Washington Carver Museum,
Tuskegee Institute National Historic Site
1212 W. Montgomery Road
Tuskegee Institute, AL 36088
334/727-3200

Exhibits that focus on Carver's far-reaching agricultural career and explore the growth of Tuskegee Institute

abolitionist
a person who supported the banning of slavery

crossbreeding
a process by which scientists create plants with specific traits, such as color or height

dehydrated
something, such as food, that has had water removed

fertilizer
a substance that adds nutrients to the soil

legume
a type of vegetable that includes peanuts, peas, and beans

midwife
a person who helps mothers deliver their babies

nutrients
chemicals necessary for healthy growth

patents
exclusive rights granted by a government to inventors to make or sell inventions

postgraduate
school work done after graduating from a college

racism
the belief that one race is better than another

segregation
the practice of separating people of different races

synthesize
to combine parts or elements to form a whole

tariff
a tax placed on goods brought into a country

Source Notes

Chapter 1

Page 9, line 8: Rackam Holt. *George Washington Carver: An American Biography.* Rev. ed. Garden City, N.Y.: Doubleday, 1963, p. 266.

Page 12, line 11: Linda O. McMurry. *George Washington Carver: Scientist and Symbol.* New York: Oxford University Press, 1981, p. 171.

Page 12, line 21: Ibid., p. 175.

Page 13, line 3: *George Washington Carver: An American Biography*, p. 267.

Chapter 2

Page 18, line 16: Gary R. Kremer. *George Washington Carver in His Own Words.* Columbia: University of Missouri Press, 1987, p. 23.

Page 18, line 17: United States Department of the Interior. National Park Service. George Washington Carver National Monument. "The Life of GWC: In His Own Words," 26 Sept. 2006, www.nps.gov/gwca/expanded/auto_bio.htm

Page 21, line 10: *George Washington Carver in His Own Words*, p. 23.

Page 25, line 2: "The Life of GWC: In His Own Words."

Page 25, line 8: Ibid.

Chapter 3

Page 28, line 4: *George Washington Carver in His Own Words*, p. 28.

Page 32, line 7: *George Washington Carver: Scientist and Symbol*, p. 22.

Page 33, line 3: Ibid., p. 23.

Chapter 4

Page 36, line 6: Ibid.

Page 37, line 5: Ibid., p. 24.

Page 37, line 17: United States Department of the Interior. National Park Service. George Washington Carver National Monument. "About GWC: A Tour of His Life." 26 Sept. 2006, www.nps.gov/gwca/expanded/gwc_tour_03.htm

Page 37, line 20: *George Washington Carver in His Own Words*, p. 21.

Page 40, line 5: *George Washington Carver: An American Biography*, p. 63.

Page 41, line 16: *George Washington Carver in His Own Words*, p. 43.

Chapter 5

Page 46, line 1: Ibid, p. 24.

Page 46, line 10: *George Washington Carver: An American Biography*, p. 74.

Page 48, line 3: *George Washington Carver in His Own Words*, p. 50.

Page 49, line 5: *George Washington Carver: Scientist and Symbol*, p. 33.

Page 49, sidebar: Mississippi State University Extension Service. "Hatch Act." 26 Sept. 2006, http://msucares.com/about_msucares/hatch.html

Page 51, line 13: *George Washington Carver in His Own Words*, p. 47.

Page 51, line 19: *George Washington Carver: An American Biography*, p. 98.

Page 52, line 15: "About GWC: A Tour of His Life," www.nps.gov/gwca/expanded/gwc_tour_04.htm

Chapter 6

Page 56, sidebar: Booker T. Washington. *Up From Slavery*. New York: Doubleday, 1998, p. xiii.

Page 56, line 26: *George Washington Carver in His Own Words*, p. 64.

Page 59, line 8: *George Washington Carver: Scientist and Symbol*, pp. 49–50.

Page 60, line 19: *George Washington Carver in His Own Words*, p. 64.

Page 63, line 2: Ibid., p. 64.

Page 63, line 14: United States Department of the Interior. National Park Service. "Legends of Tuskegee: George Washington Carver—A Great Teacher," 26 Sept. 2006, www.cr.nps.gov/museum/exhibits/tuskegee/gwcteach.htm

Page 63, lines 19 and 21: Washington, Booker T. *The Booker T. Washington Papers, Vol. 10, 1909–1911*. Champaign: University of Illinois Press, 1981. 26 Oct. 2006, www.historycooperative.org/btw/Vol.10/html/497.html

Chapter 7

Page 65, line 6: Peter Duncan Burchard. *George Washington Carver: For His Time and Ours*. United States Department of the Interior. National Park Service. 26 Sept. 2006, www.nps.gov/applications/parks/gwca/ppdocuments/Special%20History%20Study.pdf, p. 10.

Page 66, line 2: *George Washington Carver: Scientist and Symbol*, p. 130.

Page 67, line 19: Ibid., p. 86.

Page 70, line 24: *George Washington Carver in His Own Words*, p. 90.

Page 72, line 4: Ibid., pp. 85–86.

Chapter 8

Page 76, line 2: *George Washington Carver: For His Time and Ours*, p. 109.

Page 77, sidebar: *George Washington Carver in His Own Words*, p. 153.

Page 78, line 20: *George Washington Carver: An American Biography*, p. 240.

Page 80, line 3: *George Washington Carver in His Own Words*, p. 103.

Page 81, line 12: *George Washington Carver: Scientist and Symbol*, p. 199.

Page 82, line 5: Glenn Clark. *The Man Who Talks With the Flowers: The Intimate Life Story of Dr. George Washington Carver*. Saint Paul, Minn.: Macalester Park Publishing, 1939, p. 6.

Page 83, line 9: Ibid., p. 7.

Page 83, line 26: *George Washington Carver: Scientist and Symbol*, p. 220.

Chapter 9

Page 88, line 17: Ibid., p. 244.

Page 90, line 26: *George Washington Carver: For His Time and Ours*, p. 67.

Page 94, line 3: *George Washington Carver in His Own Words*, p. 128.

Select Bibliography

Burchard, Peter Duncan. *George Washington Carver: For His Time and Ours*. United States Department of the Interior, National Park Service. 2005, www.nps.gov/applications/parks/gwca/ppdocuments/Special%20History%20Study.pdf

Clark, Glenn. *The Man Who Talks with the Flowers: The Intimate Life Story of Dr. George Washington Carver*. Saint Paul, Minn.: Macalester Park Publishing, 1939.

Davis, Ronald L.F. "Creating Jim Crow." *The History of Jim Crow*. 26 Sept. 2006, www.jimcrowhistory.org/history/creating2.htm

George Washington Carver Cabin. Henry Ford Museum/Greenfield Village. 26 Sept. 2006, www.hfmgv.org/village/porchesandparlors/gwcarver/default.asp

Harlan, Louis R. *Booker T. Washington: The Making of a Black Leader*, 1856–1901. New York: Oxford University Press, 1972.

Mississippi State University Extension Service. "Hatch Act." 26 Sept. 2006, http://msucares.com/about_msucares/hatch.html

Higham, John. *Strangers in the Land: Patterns of American Nativism, 1860–1925*. New York: Atheneum, 1977.

Holt, Rackam. *George Washington Carver: An American Biography*. Rev. ed. Garden City, N.Y.: Doubleday, 1963.

Kremer, Gary R., ed. *George Washington Carver in His Own Words*. Columbia: University of Missouri Press, 1987.

McMurry, Linda O. *George Washington Carver: Scientist and Symbol*. New York: Oxford University Press, 1981.

Painter, Nell Irvin. *Creating Black Americans: African-American History and Its Meanings, 1619 to the Present*. New York: Oxford University Press, 2006.

United States Department of the Interior. National Park Service. George Washington Carver National Monument. "About GWC: A Tour of His Life." 26 Sept. 2006, www.nps.gov/gwca/expanded/gwc_tour_03.htm

United States Department of the Interior. National Park Service. "Legends of Tuskegee: George Washington Carver—A Great Teacher," 26 Sept. 2006, www.cr.nps.gov/museum/exhibits/tuskegee/gwcteach.htm

United States Department of the Interior. National Park Service. George Washington Carver National Monument. "The Life of GWC: In His Own Words." 26 Sept. 2006, www.nps.gov/gwca/expanded/auto_bio.htm

Index

About the Author

Michael Burgan is a freelance writer of books for children and adults. A history graduate of the University of Connecticut, he has written more than 100 fiction and nonfiction children's books. For adult audiences, he has written news articles, essays, and plays. Michael Burgan is a recipient of an Educational Press Association of America award.

Image Credits

The Granger Collection, New York, cover (top), 4–5, 31, 62, 98 (top left); Library of Congress, cover (bottom), 2, 24, 38, 46–47, 54, 57, 59, 64, 71, 96 (top right and bottom, all), 97 (top left and bottom), 99 (top right and bottom, all), 100 (bottom); Tuskegee University Archives, 8, 44, 73, 99 (top left), 100 (top); Corbis, 11, 13; Missouri Botanical Garden, 14, 98 (top right); George Washington Carver National Monument, 16, 19, 23, 84, 93, 96 (top left); North Wind Picture Archives, 20, 26, 68; Courtesy National Park Service, Museum Management Program and Tuskegee Institute National Historic Site, TUIN863, 29; Kansas State Historical Society, 33, 40; Simpson College Archives, 34, 82; George Washington Carver Exhibit, Ottawa County Historical Museum, Minneapolis, Kansas, 36; Iowa State University/Special Collections Department, 48, 50, 53, 61, 97 (top right); Bettmann/Corbis, 66, 76, 86, 91; Hulton Archive/Getty Images, 74; Tuskegee Institute National Historic Site, National Park Service, 79; Courtesy National Park Service, Museum Management Program and Tuskegee Institute National Historic Site, TUIN1811, 80; Hulton-Deutsch Collection/Corbis, 89; Philip LePoudre, 94, 101 (top, all); Compass Point Books, 98 (bottom left); NASA, 98 (bottom right); DVIC/NARA, 101 (bottom).